P9-DFQ-672

Coconut's
Guide to Life

Life Lessons from a Girl's Best Friend

★ American Girl™

Published by American Girl Publishing, Inc.
Copyright © 2003 by American Girl, LLC

Questions or comments? Call 1-800-845-0005,
visit our Web site at **americangirl.com**,
or write to Customer Service, American Girl,
8400 Fairway Place, Middleton, WI 53562-0497.

Printed in China
09 10 11 12 13 14 15 LEO 21 20 19 18 17 16

Editorial Development: Elizabeth Chobanian,
Kristi Thom, Michelle Watkins

Art Direction: Camela Decaire, Chris Lorette David

Design: Camela Decaire

Production: Kendra Pulvermacher,
Mindy Rappe, Cindy Hach

Illustrations: Casey Lukatz

Though just a pup and small in size,
Coconut is very wise.
She's learning lessons, as dogs do,
but they make sense for people, too.
A bit of wisdom, treat-sized tips
on life and school and true friendships.
Here's a best friend's good advice–
Coconut's golden rules for life!

Friends are everywhere—

you just have to look.

Listen with your head and heart.

Being a good listener doesn't mean you'll always know what to say. That's O.K. Sometimes a patient ear is all that's needed.

Stay Focused

Make eye contact. If your eyes are wandering, so is your attention.

In One Ear

...and out the other? A good listener concentrates on what's being said.

Ssshhh!

Try not to interrupt. Talking things out takes time.

A good friend is always there for you.

Even a perfect pup

Buried inside every mistake are the words you need to make things better—you just have to find them. When you need to apologize to someone . . .

Look the person in the eye.

Take responsibility. Don't give excuses or blame others.

Say, "I'm sorry," and mean what you say.

messes up.

Explain what you wish you had done.

Tell the person how bad you feel.

Promise you'll try not to make the same mistake again.

If someone apologizes to you, try to forgive—and forget. A good friend doesn't dig up the past.

Be
yourself...

Use Your Head . . . Follow Your Heart . . . Stand Up for What's Right

Be a

class act.

COME to class prepared. Bring homework, something to write with, and anything else you need. Make a checklist for yourself to make it easy.

SIT UP, and keep your eyes on the teacher. Slouching, fidgeting, and wiggling tell the teacher you aren't paying attention.

STAY focused on what the teacher says. If you don't understand something, ask for help.

SPEAK up in class. Know the answer? Give it. Have an opinion? Share it. Got a question? Ask it!

To get what you want . . .

keep digging.

Keep your cool
when all eyes are on you.

Whether you're giving a book report or have the lead in the school play, here's how to calm the jitters.

Practice. The more prepared you are, the more relaxed you'll be.

Breathe. Slow, deep breaths will keep your body relaxed, even when your mind is racing.

Concentrate. Think about what you're doing so you don't get distracted.

Focus. Pay attention to your performance. Don't worry about what other people are thinking.

Pretend. Try to act calm. You'll feel in control on the inside if you appear calm on the outside.

Enjoy! Nervousness is just extra energy. Use it to do your best and have fun!

A good sport

always
wins.

Have a Ball!

Play tug with a friend. Take a **walk** around the block—twice. **Wriggle** all over. **Chase** a butterfly. Discover a new way to **catch** a Frisbee. **Go** exploring. **Race** a friend around your yard. Play **hide**-and-seek. Get your pack together and **play** tag. **Dress** up. **Run** as fast as you can. **Fall** asleep in the shade. **Catch** falling raindrops on your tongue. **Imagine** something wonderful. **Watch** the clouds. **Cuddle** up with a blanket. **Sing** a song to the moon. **Dance**. Try to **find** a four-leaf clover. **Sniff** every flower along the way. **Laugh** out loud. **Save** the last treat for a friend. **Be** there for someone you love. **Share** a smile. **Dream** of faraway places. **Watch** the sun rise.

Get the giggles and **give** them to a friend. **Follow** your nose. Let yourself **get messy**. Take a long **nap** in a sunny spot. **Celebrate** for no reason. **Be** thankful. **Cheer** for the underdog. **Look** closely at a butterfly. **Try** something new. **Learn** a new trick and **teach** it to a friend. **Stick up** for a friend. **Get** your paws wet. **Come** when a friend calls. **Wish** upon a star. **Share** your treats. **Open** your heart. **Daydream**. Stop to **make** a new friend. **Think** big. **Listen**. **Stay** true to yourself. **Remember** something that makes you happy. **Try** the impossible. **Throw** a party. **Help** a friend. **Give** someone you love a hug. **Count** the leaves on a tree. See how high you can **jump**. Leave your paw **print** in the sand. **Wonder**. **Look** forward to tomorrow.

Start every day

waggin' your tail.

Hug someone you love.

Ask a friend for advice.

Play your favorite game.

Pet a pet—real or stuffed.

Ignore negative thoughts.

Nap in a sunny spot.

Exercise. A walk works wonders.

Snuggle up with something soft.

Smile at someone, and watch her smile back!

Keep Your Chin Up

Being brave isn't always easy. When you're scared silly . . .

Think Positive!
Focusing on someone you love will make you feel safer.

Breathe!
Take a deep breath, hold it for a second, then let it out. You'll feel calmer right away.

Get Going!
Doing something you enjoy will take your mind off what's scaring you.

Speak Up!
Make a little noise. Sometimes hearing your own voice makes you feel better.

Get the Giggles!
Think of something funny. Laughter always chases away the chills.

Hang in There!
Remember that tomorrow is on its way, and nothing seems as scary in the sunshine.

You're **never** too little to dream **big** dreams.

The End!

Explore the world of Coconut and American Girl

You've read all about that lovable white Westie, Coconut™. Now discover all of the dolls, outfits, and accessories available from American Girl!

Request a FREE catalogue!

Just mail this card, call 1-800-845-0005, or visit americangirl.com.

Parent's name   /   /
                                                    Girl's birth date

Address

City   State   Zip

Parent's e-mail *(provide to receive updates and Web-exclusive offers)*

(   )
Parent's phone   ❑ Home ❑ Work

Parent's signature   151964i

Send a catalogue to a grandparent or a friend:

Name

Address

City   State   Zip

        ❑ Grandparent 152633i   ❑ Friend 151967i

Today's date

Visit americangirl.com and click on **Fun for Girls** for Coconut-inspired games, quizzes, and activities!

★ **American Girl**®

PO BOX 620497
MIDDLETON WI 53562-0497

||.|..||.|.|.||...||||...|.||.|.|..||.|..|.|||